KU-711-092

Hereward College

LEARNING RESOURCES
CENTRE

00016931

BRITAIN'S CENTURY
POPULAR CULTURE

Press Association

BRITAIN'S CENTURY

POPULAR CULTURE

MAINSTREAM
PUBLISHING

EDINBURGH AND LONDON

Copyright © PA News Ltd, 1999
All rights reserved

First published in Great Britain in 1999 by
MAINSTREAM PUBLISHING COMPANY (EDINBURGH) LTD
7 Albany Street
Edinburgh EH1 3UG

ISBN 1 84018 287 3

No part of this book may be reproduced or transmitted in any form or by any
means without written permission from the publisher, except by a reviewer who
wishes to quote brief passages in connection with a review written for insertion in
a magazine, newspaper or broadcast

A catalogue record for this book is available from the British Library

Designed by Janene Reid
Typeset in Gill Sans Light
Printed and bound in Great Britain by Butler & Tanner Ltd

The crowd watching the 100 kilometres cycle race at the 1908 Olympic Games in London.

The start of the London Olympics Marathon at Windsor Castle, July 1908.

Hayes wins the Olympics Marathon, London, 1908.

Jules Gautier, the manacled swimmer, preparing to make a splash with his unusual skills.

Coasters making their way to the Derby, c. 1913.

Lady de Bathe – formerly actress and royal mistress Lillie Langtry – at work on a farm near Newmarket, Suffolk, c. 1919.

Actor Charlie Chaplin addressing a crowd outside the Ritz Hotel in London, 1921.

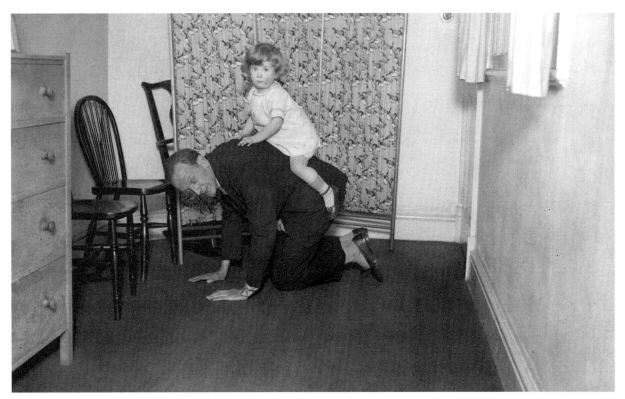

Writer A.A. Milne entertains his son Christopher Robin, in 1922, in the nursery where Winnie-the-Pooh was born.

With his lassie by his side: music hall comedian Harry Lauder and wife, leaving for a world tour, 1922.

The Duke and Duchess of York and the Fresh Air Fund children in Epping Forest, July 1923. The Duchess tries her hand at a coconut shy.

Playwright Noël Coward and actress Lilian Braithwaite leave London's Waterloo Station in April 1925, heading for the United States.

Russian ballerina Anna Pavlova photographed in the grounds of her home at Hampstead, London, July 1930.

Folk-dancing in the streets of Stratford-upon-Avon, after the Prince of Wales opened the new Shakespeare Memorial Theatre in April 1932.

Teddy Brown, the famous 22-stone xylophone player, sits astride a 147cc Coventry Eagle Silent Superb motorcycle.

Above right: High Society women Miss Margaret Whigham and Miss Holloway on Ladies' Day at Ascot, 1932.

Karl Sander, formerly a circus performer and latterly a German advertising agent, demonstrating in London his novel way of advertising – seen here riding beside a bus in Streatham, August 1932.

Viscount Lascelles' pony prior to competing in the Bramham Moor Hunt Gymkhana at Harewood Park, 1932.

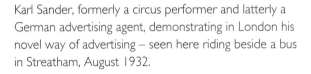

Artist Stanley Spencer at work on one of his resurrection paintings for the oratory in the village of Burghclere, Hampshire, December 1932.

Crazy Gang comics Nervo and Knox and Eddie Gray in 1932, performing their sketch 'Fun at a Petrol Station'. King George V was said to have laughed until he cried, when he saw it.

Bats and belles: actresses Flora Robson and Margery Binner go out to face the bowling during a cricket match, June 1933.

Scene inside the Catholic
Women's League canteen and
recreation hut, next door to
Westminster Cathedral, London,
maintained for members of the
British armed forces during the
Second World War.

A picture of relaxation on Bournemouth's sun-soaked beach, July 1946.

Ivor Novello presents a stage 'Oscar' in June 1947. Eileen Herlie received the Helen Perry award for best actress, for her performance in *The Eagle Has Two Heads*.

A very young Julie Andrews rehearsing in November 1948.

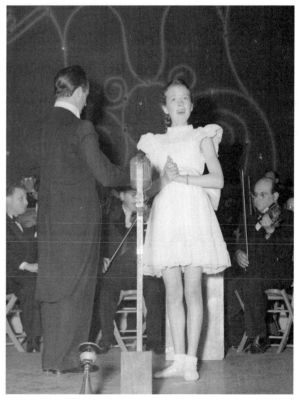

Blackpool Tower soars above the hordes of beach-seeking holidaymakers in July 1948.

Ballet star Moira Shearer at a dress rehearsal for the Sadlers Wells production of *Cinderella* at London's Covent Garden, December 1948.

Actress Elizabeth Taylor, already a film star at the age of
16, leaves London's Victoria Station on the boat train for
Paris, February 1949.

Film actress Honor Blackman riding her motor bike
through Hyde Park, London, May 1949.

Husband and wife, Sir Laurence Olivier and Vivien Leigh, attend a theatrical garden party at the Roehampton Club, London, May 1949.

Author-playwright Noël Coward seen on arrival at Southampton from New York aboard the liner *Queen Mary*, June 1949.

Actress Angela Lansbury pictured with her actor fiancé
Peter Shaw, in London, July 1949.

Film and music-hall comedian George Formby with his
wife Beryl in September 1949, bound for Canada to join
the first British company of variety artistes to tour
Canada for 20 years.

Comedian and old Etonian Michael Bentine rehearsing his act for an appearance before the King and Queen in the 1949 Royal Command Performance at the London Coliseum.

Comedy couple: Hattie Jacques and John Le Mesurier leaving Kensington register office after their wedding in London, November 1949.

Vera Lynn on stage at Grosvenor House, London, during the 1949 National Radio Awards.

A youthful-looking Richard Attenborough takes a break from film work to drive local children around the model railway at a carnival in Regent's Park, London, 1950.

A camping stand at the Festival Exhibition of Caravan Homes in London's Oxford Street, July 1951.

Pearly Kings and Queens at the 1951 South Bank Exhibition in London: Mr J. Marriott, Pearly King of Finsbury, is lighting a cigar for his wife.

Joan Collins, in September 1951, aged 18, preparing for action in her first leading screen role. The film was *One Sinner*, the location Endell Street Baths, in Holborn, London.

Above right: Character actor Terry-Thomas leaving his home in Queen's Gate Mews, London, December 1951, with a suitably caddish grin for the camera.

Norman Wisdom arriving home off a plane from New York after proving a roaring success on American TV, December 1951.

Gerald Campion, in the role of Billy Bunter, at the BBC studios in Portland Place, London, January 1952.

Muffin the Mule meets Muffin Club members in February 1952. Looking on is Annette Mills, who sang and played the piano in the popular children's TV show.

An apprentice cooper is initiated with a traditional
ceremony at the Stag Brewery, Pimlico, London, in 1952.
He was put in a barrel and covered with water and soot.

Comedy heroes Stan Laurel (Lancashire-born) and
Oliver Hardy pictured in August 1952 aboard the *Queen
Mary* at Southampton, prior to a theatre tour of Britain.

The Queen arrives for a royal film première at the Empire, Leicester Square, in October 1952.

Two competitors practise their skills for the forthcoming Transatlantic Pancake Trophy race in Olney, Buckinghamshire, January 1953.

Margaret Rutherford (left) and Carol Marsh at the Wimbledon Theatre, London, in a stage adaptation of Lewis Carroll's classic *Alice Through the Looking Glass*, February 1954.

Katie Boyle finds herself the centre of attention from comedians Norman Wisdom (left) and Al Read at the London Palladium. They were rehearsing together for the 1954 Royal Variety Performance.

Above left: With heads muffled against the cold, men from Jamaica arrive at Victoria Station, London, in search of jobs and somewhere to live. They were among 400 Jamaicans who had landed at Folkestone early in 1955 after travelling across Europe.

Actress Audrey Hepburn smiles broadly as she arrives at the Odeon, Leicester Square, London, for a film première and the presentation of the 1955 British Film Academy Awards.

Left: Actor Peter Cushing and his wife Helen at London's Heathrow Airport on their return from Madrid, June 1955.

Film star Diana Dors in a gem-embroidered gown for a celebrity appearance in London, august 1955.

Above right: Actor-writer Bryan Forbes and actress Nanette Newman leaving Caxton Hall register office, London, after their wedding ceremony in August 1955.

Mr F. Conn tends a seven-foot-tall sunflower growing on a narrow raft on the River Thames at Limehouse, east London. The plant probably sprang up from a seed dropped by a bird.

Above left: Elizabeth Voge prepares vegetables in the test meal for the Bride of the Year title at London's Royal Festival Hall, November 1955.

Saucy funnyman Benny Hill with his bloodhound Fabian in the 1956 comedy *film Who Done It?* – set at Cruft's Dog Show.

Left: Peggy Mount in 1956 with Gordon Jackson (left) and Ronald Lewis during a scene from the film *Sailor Beware*.

Hilda Baker leaving London by plane for a two-week visit to America, February 1956.

When Larry met Marilyn: Hollywood sex symbol Marilyn Monroe with Sir Laurence Olivier at the Savoy Hotel, London, in 1956. They were to star in the film *The Sleeping Prince*.

Children peer through the gates of a house in Surrey, hoping to get a glimpse of Marilyn Monroe, who was staying there with her playwright husband Arthur Miller during the summer of 1956.

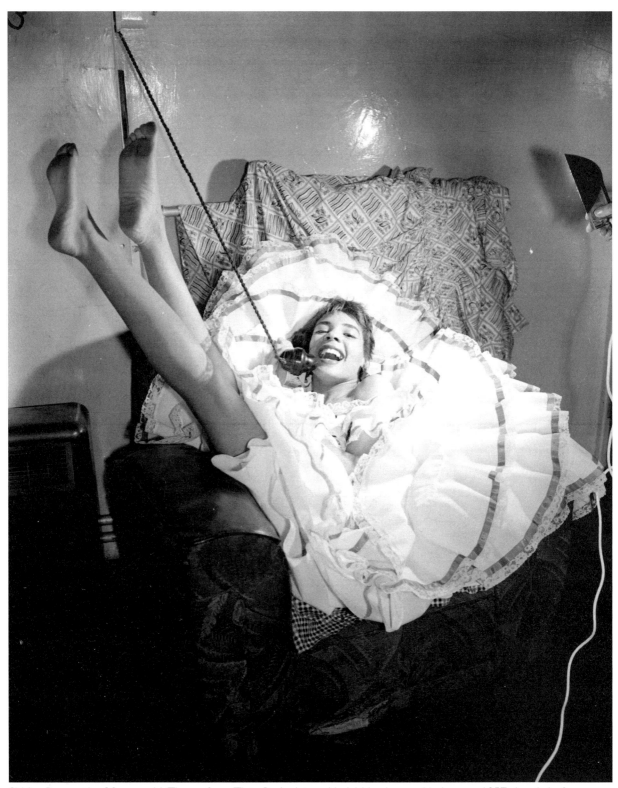

Shirley Bassey, the 20-year-old 'Tigress from Tiger Bay', pictured in laid-back mood in January 1957 shortly before jetting off to sing in Las Vegas.

Debonair Hollywood actor Cary Grant photographed n 1957, some 53 years after he was born, Archibald Leach, in Bristol.

Above right: Showbiz superstar Tommy Steele embarking on a tour of Scandinavia, September 1957.

Regent Street, London, April 1958: some of the thousands who went on a march to the Atomic Research Establishment at Aldermaston, Berkshire, in protest at the production of nuclear weapons.

British-born master of cinematic suspense Alfred Hitchcock heads for a plane to take him home to California, via Paris, March 1958.

Above right: Tony Hancock in January 1958, during rehearsals for a BBC TV version of Gogol's *The Government Inspector*.

Beside a recruiting poster, rock 'n' roll singer Marty Wilde pauses to light a cigarette as he arrives for his National Service medical examination in south London, February 1959.

Princess Margaret and Antony
Armstrong-Jones in Buckingham
Palace after their royal wedding
ceremony at Westminster Abbey
in London, May 1960.

Douglas Hoare and his daughter Patricia Ann paint a seaside telephone box in Swanage, June 1960. The pair worked locally in Hampshire and Dorset, maintaining the red kiosks for the GPO.

Prince Charles with sister
Princess Anne trying their hands
at puppetry in 1960, during a
backstage visit at London's
Victoria Palace Theatre,
following a show involving
Italian marionettes.

Preview of the 1960 International
Caravan Exhibition at Olympia,
London: models demonstrate a
special add-on tent feature for the
Sprite Countryman caravan.

'At under £300 and capable of
returning 95 mpg, this dual-
purpose Trojan three-wheel
estate van is a handy addition to
the increasing range of small cars
in this country.' Motor marketing,
1962-style.

Facing page top left: Elizabeth Taylor and Richard Burton pose for the cameras in December 1962, prior to the start of shooting for the film *The VIPs*.

Facing page top right: Cliff Richard looking reflective during rehearsals at his home, February 1963.

Facing page bottom: Stars of early-'60s TV satire *That Was The Week That Was*, showing off their tie-in LP. Left to right: William Rushton, Lance Percival, Millicent Martin, David Frost and David Kernan.

Eagerly snapped by scandal-hungry press photographers, Christine Keeler returns to the Old Bailey to give further evidence during the trial of Dr Stephen Ward, July 1963.

Mandy Rice-Davies – with Christine Keeler, a key figure in the scandal involving Cabinet Minister John Profumo – quenches her thirst for champagne at an art exhibition in London, July 1963. The portraits on show were by Dr Stephen Ward.

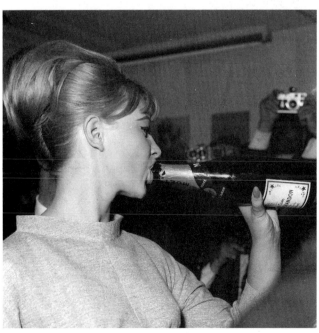

'They're fab!' Screaming fans of the Beatles watch their heroes perform in Manchester, November 1963.

The Beatles collecting for Oxfam with Jeffrey Archer (right) in their dressing-room during an interval of their December 1963 Liverpool show.

The villain is laid low during a spot of melodrama in a sketch for The Beatles' Christmas show at the Finsbury Park Astoria, London, 1963.

Joe Brown, of '60s group The Bruvvers, tries his luck on a one-armed bandit at London's Masquerade Club.

Honor Blackman (Pussy Galore) meets Sean Connery (James Bond) and quickly gets on good terms with him, during a press conference in March 1964 at Pinewood Studios for the third Bond film, *Goldfinger*.

Mods and rockers ride into town, Hastings, August 1964.

Policemen arrest a youth, summer 1964, as mods and rockers fight each other at Brighton.

Eight-year-old Andrew Tuttner meets two Daleks on Westminster Bridge, London. The robotic TV personalities were on location for a new BBC series of *Dr Who*, August 1964.

The Rolling Stones pose for a portrait, September 1964.

American civil rights leader Martin Luther King (right) takes a sunny stroll through Embankment Gardens, October 1964, during his visit to London.

Miss United Kingdom of 1964 is 20-year-old Ann Sidney, crowned at the Lyceum Ballroom, London.

Diana Rigg on a location shoot for an episode ('The Gravediggers') of cult TV series *The Avengers,* near Melton Mowbray, Leicestershire, in April 1965.

Sitting pretty, singers Cilla Black, Petula Clark and Sandie Shaw meet up at London's Dorchester Hotel in May 1965 for a record industry event.

Julie Christie and Dirk Bogarde pictured in a scene from the 1965 film *Darling*.

June 1965: Conservative MP James Dance receives from campaigner Mary Whitehouse a bundle of 366,355 signatures in support of a petition calling for the BBC 'to be asked to make a radical change of policy and produce programmes which build character instead of destroying it . . .'

Peter O'Toole (left) hands Prime Minister Harold Wilson a cup of tea, with actor Harry H. Corbett looking on, during a garden party held in July 1965 at 10 Downing Street, London.

Michael Caine – star of *Alfie*, as a fun-loving Cockney Romeo – adopts a promotional position in July 1965 at London's Dorchester Hotel. The laps belong to film co-stars (left to right) Vivien Merchant, Jane Asher, Julia Foster and Shelley Winters.

Scene inside John Stephens', one of the boutiques in Swinging London's Carnaby Street, April 1966.

Peter Cook and Dudley Moore rehearse their 'Leaping Nuns' sketch for the 1966 revue *Rustle of Spring* at the Phoenix Theatre, London.

Alf Garnet (played by Warren Mitchell, left) and his family rehearse for the Christmas 1966 episode of BBC TV's comedy *'Til Death Us Do Part*.

German actress Margit Saad (right) and Jean Herbert-Smith put the wheels on a new publicity campaign in December 1966 by towing this lightweight Sprite 400 caravan around Bryanston Square, London.

Carousel carry-on with Twiggy and Coco the Clown at the Bertram Mills Circus, Olympia, London in January 1967.

Marianne Faithfull arrives with Rolling Stone Mick Jagger for a night at the Royal Opera House in London's Covent Garden, February 1971.

Below: Speaker's Corner in Hyde Park becomes a smoker's paradise during July 1967 while London's flower children converge to take part in a 'Happening'. The crowd gathered in support of a campaign to legalise marijuana.

Oliver Reed shows a balanced approach to dog training in August 1967, during a break in filming for Lionel Bart's *Oliver.*

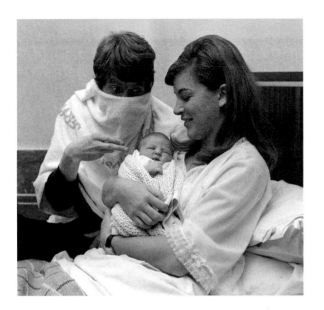

Comedian Michael
Crawford fools around
with his wife Gabrielle
and baby daughter Lucy,
December 1967.

Above right: Australian
actor George Lazenby
relaxes at a press
reception, London,
October 1968, heralding
his new role as James Bond
in the film *On Her Majesty's
Secret Service.*

A baby elephant called Eli
joins The Who aboard a
vintage French omnibus to
promote the rock band's
latest release, 'The Magic
Bus', in October 1968.

Singer Lulu with Maurice Gibb of the Bee Gees after their wedding ceremony at Gerrards Cross, Buckinghamshire, February 1969.

Beatle Paul McCartney and his American bride Linda Eastman leave Marylebone register office, London, March 1963, after tying the knot.

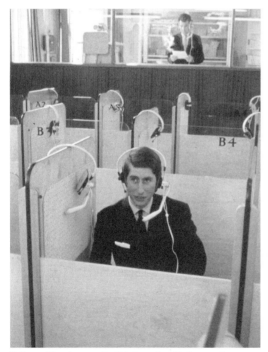

Prince Charles at the University College of Wales, Aberystwyth, April 1969.

TV presenter Hughie Green publicising his talent show *Opportunity Knocks* in 1969.

The bare-midriff look is one of many styles seen in July 1969 among the crowds gathering in Hyde Park, London, hours before a concert by the Rolling Stones.

Richard Branson at his desk in London, July 1969, when he was organiser of the Students' Advisory Service.

Australian publisher Rupert Murdoch looks at one of the first copies of his new *Sun* newspaper, November 1969.

Harry H. Corbett (right) and Wilfrid Brambell with horse Hercules for the new TV comedy *Steptoe and Son*, 1970.

Facing page top: The cast of TV series *Dad's Army* in a scene from the show. Kneeling in the foreground is Arthur Lowe, playing Captain Mainwaring.

Facing page bottom: Rome-spun humour from Frankie Howerd and a bevy of admirers in the BBC TV comedy series *Up Pompeii!* which was first broadcast in 1970.

Picture taken in February 1971 of Michael Miles on his famous TV show *Take Your Pick*.

Below left: Johnny Morris, presenter of TV's *Animal Magic*, during a visit to London Zoo, April 1971.

Circus trainer Mary Chipperfield smiles for the camera in June 1971, posing with Charles the chimpanzee.

Everything is harmonious at London's Royal Festival Hall, November 1971, as Prime Minister Edward Heath prepares to conduct the London Symphony Orchestra at a fundraising concert.

Frankie Howerd – named 1971 TV Personality of the Year by the Radio Industries Club – in distinctly French mode as an onion pedlar.

Caliper measurements are taken of veteran crime writer Agatha Christie in preparation for a wax portrait at Madame Tussaud's, London, April 1972.

The BBC *Blue Peter* line-up in May 1972: (left to right) Peter Purves, Petra, Lesley Judd, Jason, Valerie Singleton, John Noakes and Shep.

Diane Matthews burns a bra outside the Magic Circle in London, May 1972, in a women's lib gesture. She had learnt that only men are eligible to join the Circle.

Celebrity disc jockey Terry Wogan pictured at home with his family, September 1972.

Actress Vanessa Redgrave marches through London's West End in a demonstration staged by the Workers' Revolutionary Party, November 1972.

Sid James and Barbara Windsor take a break from rehearsals to parade outside the Victoria Palace in central London wearing busbies. Their revue, *Carry On London*, opened in 1973.

Paul McCartney at Heathrow Airport, December 1973, with his wife Linda and three children, Stella (being carried), Mary (centre) and Heather.

Below left: Comic duo Eric Morecambe and Ernie Wise during one of their shows at the height of their fame, May 1974.

Britt Ekland with Roger Moore before shooting begins for the James Bond film *The Man With The Golden Gun*, March 1974.

Swedish group Abba at the 1974 Eurovision Song Contest in Brighton, which they won with their entry 'Waterloo'.

Helen Morgan, Miss United Kingdom 1974, at the Royal Albert Hall, London.

Singer David Essex, pictured in July 1975.

Far right: Actor David Niven caught open-mouthed during a Foyle's luncheon in London, September 1975.

The Bay City Rollers seen on board a jumbo jet, leaving London's Heathrow airport to begin their tour of Australia, November 1975.

Mick Jagger performs with the Rolling Stones at Knebworth Park, where the legendary rock band were top of the bill. Nearly a quarter of a million fans packed the Hertfordshire site in August 1976 for the all-day concert.

Rod Stewart in full voice when more than 8,000 fervent fans packed Olympia in December 1976 for his first London concert since splitting with the Faces the previous year.

The Sex Pistols sign a new recording contract with A&M Records outside Buckingham Palace, March 1976.

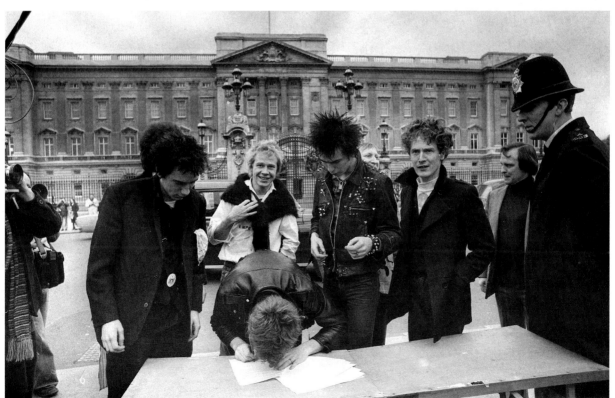

Aerial view of the big wheel and helter-skelter on the pier at Clacton, May 1978.

Habitual prisoner Norman Stanley Fletcher (Ronnie Barker, left) is doing time again for the feature film version of TV series *Porridge*, on location at Chelmsford Prison, February 1979. The picture shows co-stars Fulton Mackay (centre) and Richard Beckinsale.

ITN newsreader Anna Ford and ITN reporter Jon Snow on the day they officially announced their engagement, June 1979.

Davy Jones, who shot to fame in
the late '60s with The Monkees,
wears racing silks after taking part
in a race for amateur riders,
October 1980. Jones once
worked as a stable lad at
Newmarket.

Buck's Fizz at Heathrow airport, arriving back in the UK with their trophy after 'Making Your Mind Up' won the 1981 Eurovision Song Contest in Dublin.

'Stately homo' Quentin Crisp leaving London via Heathrow to take up residence in New York, September 1981.

Spoof band Brown Sauce celebrate the release of their record, written by BBC TV's *Multi-Coloured Swap Shop* presenter Noel Edwards (right), September 1981.

Pop idol Adam Ant (without his make-up) rehearsing for his appearance before the Queen in the Royal Variety Performance, November 1981.

Radio 1 disc jockey Dave Lee Travis in January 1982 at the Savoy Hotel, London, where he was voted Pipeman of the Year by tobacco industry workers.

A Ruritanian look for Elton John, showing off his new uniform in concert, London, October 1982.

Co-presenters of TV-AM chat among themselves on the sofa at Breakfast TV Centre, London, in February 1983. Left to right: Robert Kee, Angela Rippon, David Frost, Anna Ford and Michael Parkinson.

Actor John Wells promoting a new cigar at Harrods in London, June 1983.

Leonard Rossiter in March 1984 at the Ambassador's Theatre, London, preparing for his role as the enigmatic police inspector Truscott in Joe Orton's *Loot*.

Facing page: Policemen search a youth near the Stock Exchange, London, in late September 1984; a 'Stop the City' protest was expected to take place around this time in the form of a demonstration by various militant groups.

Right: Simon Le Bon of Duran Duran announces he is to attempt the Whitbread round-the-world yacht race, December 1984.

Boomtown Rats star Bob Geldof on stage at Wembley, 13 July 1985, during the Live Aid charity concert which he organised for famine relief in Africa.

George Michael singing at the Live Aid concert, Wembley, 1985.

Alison Moyet and Paul
Young contribute to Live
Aid at Wembley.

Freddie Mercury, lead singer
with the rock group Queen,
during Live Aid.

Far right: Sixties pop star
Dusty Springfield singing to a
1985 audience in London's
Hippodrome.

Eric Clapton in concert in Helsinki, Finland, during his 1985 tour.

Far left: Rare ends! Michael Barrymore and Anneka Rice celebrate winning the 1986 Rear of the Year competition.

David Bowie attends a London press conference in March 1987 to promote his forthcoming World Tour For AIDS campaign.

Facing page top: Radio celebrities John Peel (left) and Alan Freeman at Ronnie Scott's club, London, March 1988. Peel received a Radio Academy award for his outstanding contribution to UK music radio.

Facing page bottom: A portrait of Craig Logan and twins Matt (centre) and Luke Goss from boy band Bros, May 1988.

The Duchess of York (left) and the Princess of Wales poke some fun with their umbrellas during a wet Ladies' Day at Royal Ascot, 1987.

Prince Edward arriving at the aptly named Palace Theatre in London's West End, to start work as a production assistant with Andrew Lloyd Webber's Really Useful Theatre Company, February 1988.

Dr Who actor Jon Pertwee in London to promote a stage production of the long-running BBC TV series in February 1989.

Former *Neighbours* stars Jason Donovan and Kylie Minogue – now in singing careers – rehearse at the Dominion Theatre, London, for the 1989 Children's Royal Variety Performance.

Band members of Take That pictured at the Hard Rock Café in London, January 1993.

Politician John Prescott in performance on stage at the Red Revue in Brighton, during the 1993 Labour Party conference.

Above right: Actress Emma Thompson, who won the Oscar for Best Actress for her performance in *Howards End*, arrives at the 1993 BAFTA awards with her actor husband Kenneth Branagh.

Bristol, March 1994: Angela Berners-Wilson breaks the bread during the service at St Paul's Church, Clifton, when the Church of England's first women priests were ordained.

Above right: Jarvis Cocker during a press conference, March 1996. The metropolitan police had just decided not to take any action against him after his stage antics at the Brit Awards when he disrupted Michael Jackson's routine.

Diana, Princess of Wales, wearing a black pleated chiffon dress by Christina Stamboulian, during a party given at the Serpentine Gallery, London, 1996.

Absolutely Fabulous star Joanna Lumley makes use of one of BT's new payphones in a promotional shot, May 1996.

Above left: Paula Yates arriving at the High Court in June 1996 for the start of her legal wrangle with former husband Bob Geldof over her divorce settlement.

Blur's Damon Albarn in the spotlight as the band launch their first tour in over a year at the Mayfair Club, Newcastle, January 1997.

Media celebrities Danny Baker (left) and Chris Evans join England footballer Paul Gascoigne (right) at the 1997 TV and Radio Industries Club awards ceremony.

Designer Vivienne Westwood makes a triumphant return to Britain in February 1997, applauded by her models at the end of the catwalk show for her autumn/winter collection.

Below left: Spice Girls Geri and Victoria perform with the group on stage at the 1997 Brit Awards, where they grabbed honours for the Best British Video and Best Single.

Ralph Fiennes, star of *The English Patient*, poses for the press as he arrives at the Shrine Auditorium in Los Angeles for the 1997 Academy Awards ceremony.

The Spice Girls discover Prince Charles's Heir style at the Royal Gala, Manchester, celebrating the 21st anniversary of the Prince's Trust, 1997.

Music fans revel in the mud pools at Glastonbury, June 1997. The festival was almost called off because of recent heavy rainfall.

A young girl parades her costume at the 1997 Notting Hill Carnival, west London, on the last day of Europe's largest street festival.

Right: Supermodel Kate Moss (centre) jokes with Jade Jagger – daughter of Rolling Stone Mick Jagger – during a break in London Fashion Week, 1997.

Naomi Campbell goes for the swing in a cream dress from Amaya Arzuaga's spring/summer collection during the last day of London Fashion Week, 1997.

The Teletubby toys which featured in the Toy Fair at Earl's Court, London, October 1997. In an extraordinary genetic mix-up in Toyland, it seemed that one of the BBC's hit Teletubby characters, Dipsy (second left), had turned black.

Prince Harry enjoys the company of Spice Girls (left to right) Mel B, Emma and Victoria. He attended their concert in Johannesburg, South Africa, in November 1997.

Victoria Adams (Posh Spice) and Manchester United footballer David Beckham leave the hotel near Crewe where the announcement of their future wedding was made, January 1998.

Veteran Welsh singer Tom Jones
performs on stage in July 1998 at an
outdoor concert in Hyde Park, London,
which was held in aid of the Prince's
Trust.

TV personality Ulrika Jonsson with her
son Cameron at a film première in
London's Leicester Square, July 1998.

A London tramp moves his possessions in a very large trolley, July 1998.

Sir Anthony Hopkins looks across a rain-drenched Snowdon in August 1998, having donated £1 million to help buy the mountain which was up for sale.

Below left: Tablets of Viagra, shown in summer 1998 when the anti-impotence drug first popped up in Britain.

Film actress Kate Winslet with her new husband Jim Threapleton during their wedding reception at a pub in Stoke Row, Oxfordshire, November 1998.

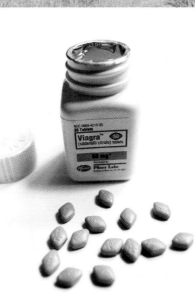

The Angel of the North statue in Gateshead with its creator Anthony Gormley. The sculptor won an award for Visual Arts at the 1999 South Bank Show in London.

Former Take That warbler Robbie Williams on stage during the 1999 Brit Awards at the London Arena. Robbie won awards for Best British Single, Best British Male Solo Artist and Best British Video.

Actress and singer Grace Jones models a hat created by designer Philip Treacy as part of London Fashion Week, 1999.

Above left: Liam Gallagher of Oasis makes a familiar gesture to the media in February 1999 as he arrives for the opening of designer Tommy Hilfiger's new flagship store in New Bond Street, London.

Dame Judi Dench with her Oscar for Best Supporting Actress at the 1999 Academy Awards, Los Angeles. She won the award for her role as Elizabeth I in *Shakespeare in Love*.

A demonstrator brandishes his 'bong' at a festival held on London's Clapham Common supporting the end of cannabis prohibition, May 1999.